AUBURN TIGERS

BY CRAIG ELLENPORT

Published by The Child's World®
1980 Lookout Drive • Mankato, MN 56003-1705
800-599-READ • www.childsworld.com

Copyright ©2022 by The Child's World®
All rights reserved. No part of this book may be reproduced or utilized in any form or by any means without written permission from the publisher.

Photos Cover: AP Photo/Roger Steinman
Interior: AP Images: Rob Carr 12. Newscom: Art Foxall/UPI 11; John Korduner/Icon SW 15; Ed Nessen/Sporting News 16; Mark LoMoglio/Icon Sportswire. Shutterstock: Critical Labz 19. Wikimedia: Tom Key 4; 7 (2); 8.

ISBN 9781503850415 (Reinforced Library Binding)
ISBN 9781503850569 (Portable Document Format)
ISBN 9781503851320 (Online Multi-user eBook)
LCCN: 2021930288

Printed in the United States of America

Touchdown! Time for the Auburn Tigers to celebrate.

CONTENTS

Why We Love College Football 4

CHAPTER ONE
Early Days 6

CHAPTER TWO
Glory Years 9

CHAPTER THREE
Best Year Ever! 10

CHAPTER FOUR
Auburn Traditions 13

CHAPTER FIVE
Meet the Mascot 14

CHAPTER SIX
Top Auburn QBs 17

CHAPTER SEVEN
Other Auburn Heroes 18

CHAPTER EIGHT
Recent Superstars 21

Glossary 22
Find Out More 23
Index 24

WHY WE LOVE COLLEGE FOOTBALL

It's fall in the South. That means one thing—college football! There are no pro football teams in Alabama. But there are millions of football fans. Many of them root for the Auburn University Tigers. Auburn is one of the most successful teams in college football history!

When Saturday arrives, the fans put on their team colors. They fill the stadium and cheer on their team. Let's meet the Tigers!

Fans fill the stands at Auburn with orange and blue, the school colors.

CHAPTER ONE

Early Days

Auburn began playing football in 1892. The team's first big year was 1913. The Tigers went 8-0. They outscored opponents 224-13! The star of that team was Kirk Newell. After college, Newell became a hero in World War I.

> **BIG CITY!**
> Auburn, Alabama, is home to about 65,000. It is the eighth-largest city in Alabama. When Auburn plays at home, there are more than 90,000 fans in the stadium. On those days, the stadium is the fifth-largest city in the state!

In 1932, Auburn joined the Southeastern **Conference** (SEC). The SEC is the sport's strongest conference. That means Auburn has a hard schedule every year!

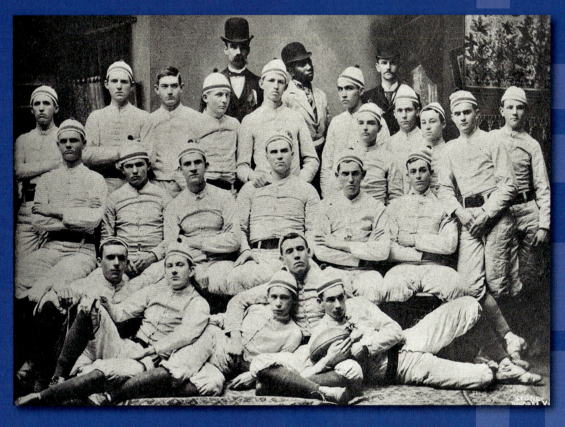

Above: Auburn's first team poses in their uniforms (but they didn't wear the caps during games!).

Right: The 1895 team takes a break from practice. The big A's are for Auburn.

Receiver Lloyd Nix catches a pass during a 1957 Auburn game.

CHAPTER TWO

Glory Years

In 1957, the Tigers tied for the college football national championship. (They shared it with Ohio State.) Coach Ralph Jordan's team had a tough defense. Auburn finished with a 10-0 record. In six of the team's wins, they didn't allow a single point. Auburn finished a perfect season by beating **rival** Alabama, 40-0!

Overall, Auburn has had 12 undefeated seasons. They have won the SEC 16 times.

> **TWO-WAY STAR**
>
> In the 1960s, football players played both offense and defense. Auburn's Tucker Frederickson was a great two-way player. In 1964, he was a member of the **All-America** team at both running back and defensive back!

CHAPTER THREE

Best Year Ever!

In 2010, quarterback Cam Newton and the Tigers were 12–0. Newton won the Heisman Trophy. That award is given to college football's best player. The Auburn defense was also very good. Nick Fairley won the Lombardi Award. That award is given to the best **defensive lineman** in the country.

AUBURN'S HEISMAN TROPHY WINNERS
Pat Sullivan, 1971
Bo Jackson, 1985
Cam Newton, 2010

In the SEC Championship Game, Auburn beat South Carolina. That earned Auburn a spot in the Bowl Championship Series. The Tigers played the Oregon Ducks for the national title.

Newton played great. The defense stopped a strong Oregon offense. Auburn won, 22-19. The Tigers were national champions!

After leaving Auburn, Newton was a star in the NFL. He led the Carolina Panthers to a spot in Super Bowl 50.

CHAPTER FOUR

Auburn Traditions

Auburn's home games are always special. Game days begin with a tradition for both players and fans. The team gathers at the Auburn athletic building. They walk to the stadium together. The tradition is called the "Tiger Walk."

As the team walks, thousands of fans line the street. They cheer as the players march past. Before kickoff, the fans follow the team into the stadium. Then they root for their Tigers!

> **THE BIG RIVAL**
>
> The state of Alabama has two big football schools. One is Auburn. The other is the University of Alabama. The two play each other in the season's final game. They have faced off every year since 1948. The game is known as "The Iron Bowl."

◄ *It's a sea of orange during the Tiger Walk! The players high-five students as they walk toward the stadium for the game.*

CHAPTER FIVE

Meet the Mascot

Auburn's mascot is Aubie the Tiger. A costumed student in a tiger suit dances at games and helps fans cheer.

The school also a famous **battle cry**. Fans yell, "War Eagle!" Nobody is sure exactly how or when this cheer started. One story is about an Auburn student who fought in the **Civil War**. He found an injured eagle and nursed it to health. Later, he brought the eagle to Auburn's first football game.

Now, a trained eagle flies in a circle around the stadium. The crowd goes crazy! They all shout, *"War Eagle!"*

The first Aubie was drawn by an artist in 1959. Aubie was just a cartoon for a long time. A costumed Aubie started coming to games in 1979.

CHAPTER SIX

Top Auburn QBs

Pat Sullivan played quarterback for Auburn from 1969 to 1971. He finished his career with 53 touchdown passes. That is a team record! In 1971, Sullivan won the Heisman Trophy.

In 1993, QB Stan White led Auburn to an undefeated season. White finished with a school-record 8,016 passing yards.

In 1997, Dameyune Craig had 3,277 passing yards. That set the school's single-season record. Craig led Auburn to a big victory over Clemson in the Peach Bowl.

> **HE DID IT ALL!**
>
> Some quarterbacks are very good passers. Some are very good runners. In 2010, Auburn's Cam Newton was great at both. He threw 30 touchdown passes and ran for 20 scores.

◄ Left, Dameyune Craig was a starter for four seasons at Auburn.

CHAPTER SEVEN

Other Auburn Heroes

Bo Jackson was one of the best all-around athletes ever. Jackson holds the Auburn career rushing record with 4,303 yards. In 1985, he won the Heisman Trophy. Jackson was later a star in the NFL and Major League Baseball.

Auburn has had many great defensive players. **Linebacker** Kevin Greene was the SEC Defensive Player of the Year in 1984. He was later elected to the Pro Football Hall of Fame.

Defensive lineman Tracy Rocker was a two-time member of the All-America team. In 1988, he won the Lombardi Award. He also won the Outland Trophy. That award is for the best defensive tackle in the country.

> **DOUBLE TROUBLE**
> Auburn was undefeated in 2004. They had awesome running backs. Carnell Williams had 1,165 rushing yards and 12 touchdowns. Ronnie Brown had 913 rushing yards and 8 touchdowns. Both went on to play in the NFL.

Huge banners at Auburn Stadium honor Tigers heroes. This banner shows Bo Jackson, the great running back.

CHAPTER EIGHT

Recent Superstars

Auburn fans have watched great players in recent years. The Tigers reached a **bowl game** every season but one from 2010 to 2020. The 2017 team finished 10-4. They were No. 10 in the country. Running back Kerryon Johnson ran for 1,391 yards and 18 touchdowns. In 2018, he was **drafted** by the Detroit Lions.

In 2019, Tigers defensive tackle Derrick Brown was named the SEC Defensive Player of the Year. In 2020, he was drafted by the NFL's Carolina Panthers.

Bo Nix took over as Auburn's starting quarterback as a **freshman** in 2019. In his first two seasons at Auburn, he had 28 touchdown passes.

Who will be the next star to add to Auburn's great history?

← Left, Bo Nix follows a tradition of great Auburn QBs.
Like Cam Newton, he's a good runner. Nix has 14 rushing TDs.

GLOSSARY

All-America (ALL uh-MAYR-ih-kuh) an honor given to players that experts consider the best players in a given year

battle cry (BAT-ul KRY) inspired by soldiers' yells, these are cheers at sports events

bowl game (BOWL GAYM) a bonus game played after a college team's regular season

Civil War (SIH-vul WAR) a conflict between Union states and Confederate states in the United States from 1861 to 1865

conference (KON-fur-enss) a group of sports teams that play each other

defensive lineman (dee-FEN-siv LYNE-man) one of three or four players on defense that play up on the line of scrimmage

drafted (DRAF-ted) chosen to play for an NFL team

freshman (FRESH-mun) a student in his or her first year at a school

linebacker (LYNE-bak-er) defensive position that plays behind the defense line and in front of the defensive backs

rival (RYE-vul) a team's main competitor

FIND OUT MORE

IN THE LIBRARY

Holmes, Parker. *The Auburn Tigers*. New York, NY: PowerKids Press, 2013.

Jacobs, Greg. *The Everything Kids' Football Book*. Avon, MA: Adams Media, 2018.

Ramey, Temple. *Auburn Tigers*. New York, NY: Weigl, 2019.

Sports Illustrated for Kids. *The Greatest Football Teams of All Time*. New York, NY: Sports Illustrated Kids, 2018.

ON THE WEB

Visit our website for links about the
Auburn Tigers:
childsworld.com/links

Note to Parents, Teachers, and Librarians: We routinely verify our Web links to make sure they are safe and active sites. So encourage your readers to check them out!

INDEX

Aubie the Tiger 14
Bowl Championship
    Series 10
Brown, Derrick 21
Brown, Ronnie 18
Carolina Panthers 10, 21
Clemson 17
Craig, Dameyune 17
Fairley, Nick 10
Fredrickson, Tucker 9
Greene, Kevin 18
Heisman Trophy 10, 17, 18
Iron Bowl 13
Jackson, Bo 10, 18, 19
Johnson, Kerryon 21
Jordan, Ralph 9

Lombardi Award 10, 18
Newell, Kirk 6
Newton, Cam 10, 17, 21
Nix, Bo 21
Nix, Lloyd 8
Ohio State 9
Oregon Ducks 10
Peach Bowl 17
South Carolina 10
Southeastern Conference
    (SEC) 6, 9, 10, 18, 21
Sullivan, Pat 10, 17
Tiger Walk 13
White, Stan 17
Williams, Carnell 18
World War I 6

ABOUT THE AUTHOR

Craig Ellenport is the author of many sports books for young readers. He went to Northwestern University, but his Wildcats didn't quite make it into this series!